THE MIRACLE OF THE BREAD, THE FISH AND THE BOY

Anthony DeStefano

Illustrated by
Richard Cowdrey

HARVEST kids

HARVEST HOUSE PUBLISHERS
EUGENE, OREGON

To Peggy and Bill Larcheid. This is a book about generosity, and you are two of the most generous people in the world. Thanks for all you do!

—Anthony DeStefano

To Hayla, Daisy, Chloe, and Rebekah. "Trust in the Lord with all your heart"!

—Richard Cowdrey

THE MIRACLE OF THE BREAD, THE FISH, AND THE BOY

Text copyright © 2018 by Anthony DeStefano • Artwork copyright © 2018 by Richard Cowdrey

Published by Harvest House Publishers Eugene, Oregon 97402 • www.harvesthousepublishers.com

HARVEST KIDS is a registered trademark of The Hawkins Children's LLC. Harvest House Publishers, Inc., is the exclusive licensee of the federally registered trademark HARVEST KIDS.

ISBN 978-0-7369-6859-1 (hardcover) • ISBN 978-0-7369-7120-1 (eBook)

Library of Congress Cataloging-in-Publication Data
Names: DeStefano, Anthony, author. | Cowdrey, Richard, illustrator.
Title: The miracle of the bread, the fish and the boy / Anthony DeStefano; illustrated by Richard Cowdrey.
    Description: Eugene, Oregon : Harvest House Publishers, [2018] | Summary: Coming home from buying his mother's birthday present, a young boy follows a crowd to hear a preacher, then gives all he has to help feed the people in this retelling of the miracle of the loaves and fishes.
Identifiers: LCCN 2017028143 (print) | LCCN 2017039714 (ebook) | ISBN 9780736971201 (ebook) | ISBN 9780736968591 (hardcover)
Subjects: LCSH: Jesus Christ—Miracles—Juvenile fiction. | Feeding of the five thousand (Miracle)—Juvenile fiction. | CYAC: Jesus—Miracles—Fiction. | Feeding of the five thousand (Miracle)—Fiction. | Generosity—Fiction. | Faith—Fiction. | Mothers and sons—Fiction.
Classification: LCC PZ7.D466 (ebook) | LCC PZ7.D466 Mir 2018 (print) | DDC [E]—dc23
LC record available at https://lccn.loc.gov/2017028143

For more information about Anthony DeStefano, please visit his website: www.anthonydestefano.com

Cover and interior design by Left Coast Design

Scripture quotations are taken from the Holy Bible, New International Version®, NIV®. Copyright © 1973, 1978, 1984, 2011 by Biblica, Inc.® Used by permission. All rights reserved worldwide.

Printed in China

17 18 19 20 21 22 23 24 25 26 / LP / 10 9 8 7 6 5 4 3 2 1

FROM THE GOSPEL OF JOHN

Then Jesus went up on a mountainside and sat down with his disciples…

When Jesus looked up and saw a great crowd coming toward him, he said to Philip, "Where shall we buy bread for these people to eat?"…

Another of his disciples, Andrew, Simon Peter's brother, spoke up, "Here is a boy with five small barley loaves and two small fish, but how far will they go among so many?"

Jesus said, "Have the people sit down." There was plenty of grass in that place, and they sat down (about five thousand men were there). Jesus then took the loaves, gave thanks, and distributed to those who were seated as much as they wanted. He did the same with the fish.

When they had all had enough to eat, he said to his disciples, "Gather the pieces that are left over. Let nothing be wasted." So they gathered them and filled twelve baskets with the pieces of the five barley loaves left over by those who had eaten.

John 6:3-13

Seven dollars and
forty-seven cents!

The little boy could
hardly believe it.

He looked down and counted the money again.
$7.47—and he had saved it all by himself!

It had taken him a
long time, but
he had managed
to do it by helping people in his town carry their
packages, by doing extra
chores around the
house, and by
never spending
even a penny of the
tiny allowance his mother
gave him.

He had saved the money for one reason—to buy his mother a special present for her birthday.

You see, the little boy lived in a fishing village by a lake with only his mother and brothers. He had no father, and his family was very poor. His mother had to work long hours just to put food on the table.

But one day the boy had an idea: If he could save enough money, maybe he could buy his family a week's worth of food,

and his mother would be able to stay home for a few days and rest her tired feet.

So the boy saved his pennies and nickels for months. Finally, on the morning of his mother's birthday, he got up extra early—just as the sun was rising—and walked to the village market by himself.

"If only I can buy the food and bring it back home before my mother wakes up," he thought. "She'll be so surprised."

When he got to the food market, he went straight through the door and reached up high to put his money on the counter. Then he boldly said to the shopkeeper: "May I have a week's worth of fish and bread, please?"

The shopkeeper was a mean-looking old man. He counted the money slowly and said in a grumpy, gravelly voice, "This is only $7.47—you expect to buy a week's worth of food with this?"

"Why not?" asked the boy. "Isn't that enough?"

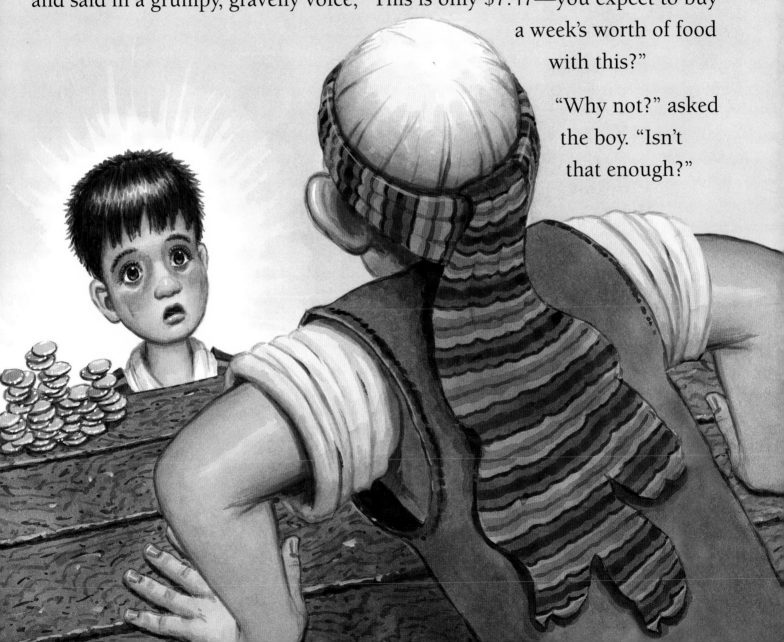

The old man squinted his eyes and growled, "Why, it's hardly any money at all!" He turned around and walked to the back of the store. In a few seconds, he returned with two fish and five small loaves of bread. He plopped them down on the counter in front of the boy.

"That's all your money will buy," he said harshly.

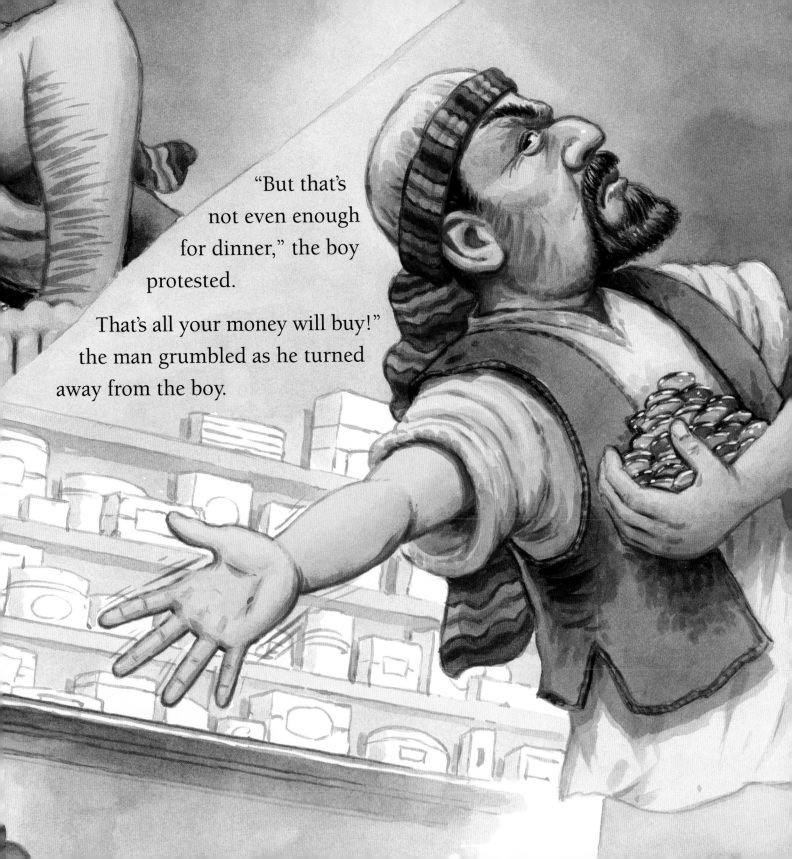

"But that's not even enough for dinner," the boy protested.

That's all your money will buy!" the man grumbled as he turned away from the boy.

The boy left the shop feeling heartbroken. He carried the fish and bread in a small basket under his arm, his head hanging low. "Now what am I going to do?" he sobbed.

"I worked so hard. I thought I had saved up a treasure. But now I don't have any money and hardly any food, and my mother won't be able to stay home from work even one day. I'm just a failure."

But as the boy walked home, he noticed a crowd of people gathering a short distance away. There were old people, young people, rich people, poor people, sick people, handicapped people —*thousands* of people—and all of them were making their way up the side of a large, sloping hill.

The boy asked someone what all the commotion was about.

"Haven't you heard? The great teacher from Nazareth is here—and He's healing the sick and preaching about God."

The boy strained his neck but couldn't see over the heads of the crowd. In fact, the swarm was so thick that he could barely move. So crouching low, he began to go through the people's legs. Because he was so small, he was able to move quickly, and before long he was close to the edge of the crowd.

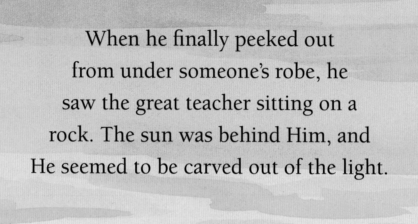

When he finally peeked out
from under someone's robe, he
saw the great teacher sitting on a
rock. The sun was behind Him, and
He seemed to be carved out of the light.

The boy listened to the man speak.
He didn't sound like most other adults
the boy knew. His words were so simple,
and yet they seemed so wise.

Just then one of the men who was with the teacher saw the boy and pulled him up by his sleeves.

He brought him over to the teacher and said, "Lord, this boy has five loaves of bread and two fish."

The teacher looked down and said, "Little boy, there are thousands of people here, and they are very hungry. Will you give Me your bread and fish so I can feed them?"

The boy was confused. "But how can You do that?" he asked. "This food that I bought isn't even enough to give my family. How can it feed this big crowd?"

The teacher smiled gently and spoke to him in a quiet voice, "Little boy, don't you know that with God all things are possible? Don't you know that if you offer everything you have to God, He will multiply all the good things you do?"

The boy remembered what his mother had taught him about God. He nodded his head and answered, "Yes, I know that God can do anything."

The teacher stretched out
his hand and asked the
boy once again for his
basket of bread and fish.

The boy
thought for a
second and
decided to
trust the man.

He gave Him all
that he had.

The man took the food and
said a short prayer of thanks.
He told the crowd to sit down
and laid the basket on the ground.
Then He closed his eyes. Suddenly,
the boy heard a low rumbling sound. It
started quietly, but it grew louder and louder.
Soon it seemed as if the earth was shaking
under his feet.

Just then the boy noticed that instead of one basket of bread and fish, there were two. Then there were four. Then eight. Then ten. In no time at all there were hundreds of baskets on the ground containing thousands of fish and loaves of bread. The boy couldn't believe his eyes. It was a miracle!

The men who were standing near the teacher began to give the food to the people in the crowd. Everyone ate until they were full. When they were finally done, there were twelve baskets of bread and fish left over.

Then the teacher said to the boy, "Remember, without God you can do nothing. But when you pray and ask God for help, He will bless all that you do and give you the power to do incredible things."

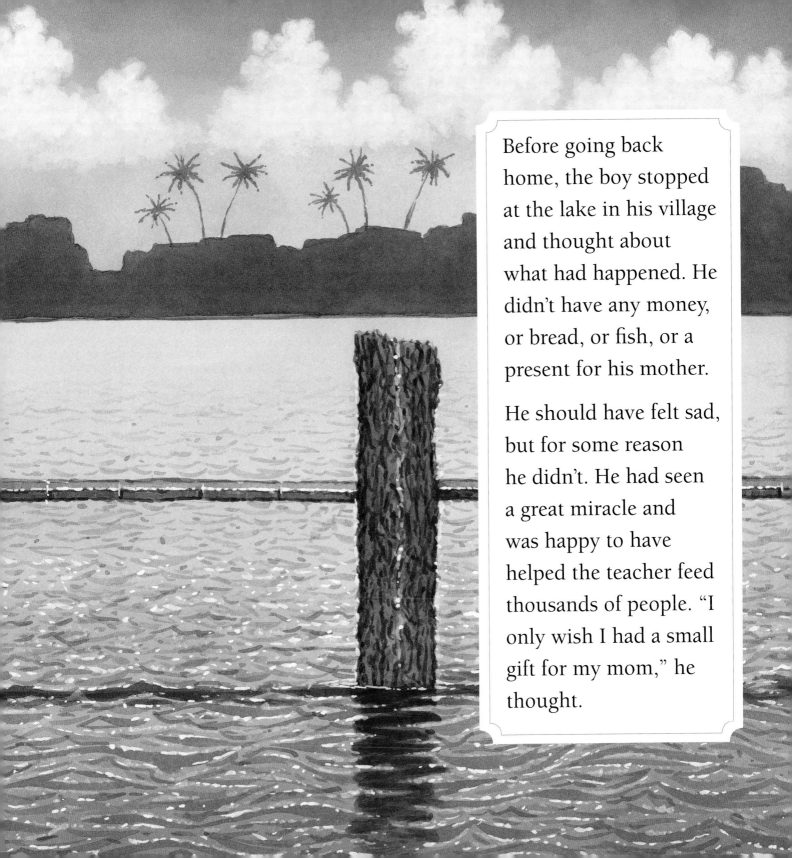

Before going back home, the boy stopped at the lake in his village and thought about what had happened. He didn't have any money, or bread, or fish, or a present for his mother.

He should have felt sad, but for some reason he didn't. He had seen a great miracle and was happy to have helped the teacher feed thousands of people. "I only wish I had a small gift for my mom," he thought.

But when he got home, an amazing surprise awaited him.

His mother rushed over to him in excitement. She pointed to a huge basket of bread and fish in the corner. "Some men came by just now and dropped off this basket," she cried. "It's enough food to last us a whole month! The men told me that they were giving it to you because you helped them today."

The boy remembered the leftover baskets of food and smiled. He looked at his mother and said, "It's not for me, Mom. It's for you. It's your birthday present. Now you can finally stay home from work and rest a while."

His mother
had tears of
joy in her eyes.
"This is the best
present anyone has
ever given me," she
said, and hugged her
son tightly.